Wealth —Over— Riches

10 Principles to Shift from
Looking Rich to Building Wealth Habits

ASHAUNDA M. DAVIS

Designed and Printed By:
Custom Made For You
graphic design & printing studio
www.custommadeforyou.net

ISBN 978-1-7326439-0-1

DEDICATION

This book is dedicated to my children—my nieces and nephews, birthed from my siblings. Particularly, I am referring to my oldest niece and nephew because I have played more of an active role in assisting with raising and being a care-giver for them. Now to my two younger nieces and nephew, Auntie truly loves and cares for you also. This book is meant to inspire each of you to achieve greatness. See, I believe that we should be an example for someone, if not ourselves, as well as leave a legacy.

Accordingly, since I do not have any children of my own as yet, when I reminisce about your upbringing, you both make my heart smile, and tears immediately come to my eyes. I was there for your births, changed your diapers, crawled on the floor with you, and chased you across the hall (from room to room, upstairs in Granddad and Duchess' house). My prayer is that DESPITE any challenges, missing persons in your life, and/or negative issues life throws your way, you'll look deep inside yourself, tap into the prayer and power of the God inside you, get up, and MAKE YOUR MARK on this planet! YOUR LIFE is worth much more than you might imagine right now. I love you, Desmond Wilson, Ja'hdai Davis-McCarty, Zoie Wilson, Alannah Wilson, and Robert Cerullo.

W
R

Table of Contents

W
R

PREFACE

Do you see them? Can you see the men and women dressed to the nines; wearing the latest designer outfits, shoes, shades, hats, and watches; and driving the latest edition, fully-loaded, foreign-made automobile? They have all the trappings of a lavish lifestyle, but if you were to dig deeper, six times out of ten, you would find that they live paycheck to paycheck. They tend to average around $137,063 of debt, with a median income of only $59,039, less than $1,700 in regular savings, and under $63,000 saved for retirement. You see, it is all about the "look" of wealth—if you look rich, you must be rich, right? WRONG!

My name is Ashaunda Davis. I am a professional financial advisor and coach. My mission is to teach people how to actually BE wealthy by creating wealth mindsets, behaviors, and HABITS. In addition, I want to show teens and professionals how to manage money so effectively that living a life of luxury does not come with the stress and strain of wondering how they are going to make the next lease payment on that Benz or avoid the embarrassment of having their Black Card denied.

W
R

CHAPTER
ONE
Lessons Learned

"Financial Freedom is available to those who desire to learn about it and work for it."
Ashaunda Davis

I remember waking up on Saturday mornings, getting out of bed, and making my way down our winding staircase, without a real care in the world. I'd find my parents sitting at the kitchen table, staring at a pile of paper stacked on the table.

After "Good mornings" were exchanged, I'd ask, "What are you guys doing?"

They'd respond, "Going over our budget and paying bills."
I'd get on my knees on one of the kitchen chairs, elbows on the table and leaning forward, trying to understand the totally unfamiliar terms I saw on the papers. They'd ask if I wanted to help, and I'd of course reply, "Yes"—proud to be a part of what was undeniably an important adult activity. They even allowed me to write out the checks. To this day, I'm sure there were clerks at many of the companies who wondered what was going on in our house. But who could blame them? After all,

they received checks that were written in what was obviously a child's handwriting.

The lessons I learned sitting at that table with my parents—carefully writing out checks and listening as they discussed the budget, what money needed to go where, how we were doing financially as a family, and so on—resonates with me to this present day. I learned the importance of slowing down, deliberately taking a look at my responsibilities, and then diligently managing them. I discovered how meaningful it is to a relationship for both parties to come together over money management and their willingness to pass that skill on to the next generation, by engaging them in the process.

Being educated in financial management at such a tender age set a foundation that allowed me to successfully manage my money—from when I worked my first job as a retail clerk, through college, where I worked upwards of three jobs in order to cover my expenses. I carried those lessons on through the lean years as a struggling entrepreneur to now, as I continue to build my business empire.

Discovering My Calling

I grew up around people who ran network marketing businesses of all kinds. Consequently, I had access to a number of professional development books and tapes. I was also able to attend motivational conventions, where I heard speakers of all levels espousing that the best thing for anyone to do was to find a job they'd be willing to do for free and discover a way to get paid well to do it.

Without knowing it at the time, that's exactly what I had begun to do. While I was in my twenties, friends, colleagues, and/or family members would often ask me to help them set up their budgets. I'm not sure what it was they saw in me, but whatever it was, it led them to my door. I was more than willing to provide this service to them for free at the time; after all, I had already developed a passion for teaching people the valuable lessons I had learned while sitting with my parents at our kitchen table.

After earning my Masters in Communications Studies and Business, I landed a job teaching business principles at my old high school. I was finally being paid for my expertise, but beyond that, I was proud to be back at my old school in a position that allowed me to influence the next generation, through a relationship of trust and engagement—much like I'd had with my parents.

During this time, I was also building a network marketing business of my own. I was helping provide everyday adults with access to quality legal counsel they might have otherwise not been able to afford. It wasn't long before I became known within the organization as an industry expert. I was consistently being invited to lead corporate teleconferences or give weekly presentations. I was rewarded with all-expense-paid, luxury trips to exotic destinations, as a member of the "elite" leadership team.

I realized at that point that there was money to be made in offering clients a full suite of products. In addition to marketing legal counsel, I could provide insurances for other areas of their lives—life, property, and casualty to name a few. I studied diligently to earn my insurance licenses and added that to my list of accomplishments and services.

It took me eight short years to recognize that at the core of all I'd done career-wise, to that point, was a certain level of financial advisement. Starting with those friends and family members, right up to the clients who came to me for life insurance, underneath it all, there were discussions of budgeting, financial planning, and being able to afford it all.

It took no time at all to earn my Financial Advisor designations, with a few special designations left to obtain. I went from offering free budget advice at people's kitchen tables to helping CEOs and entrepreneurs secure their businesses' financial futures. I was finally a Professional Financial Advisor!

Finding My Niche

My first full year as a full-fledged Financial Advisor brought me mostly female clients who, during our initial consultations (what I like to call the "Simple Financial Conversation"), would be moved to tears. I would ask them general questions about their current finances—if they currently had control of their finances, had stable savings, and/or were prepared for the future lifestyle in their retirement years. Their answers were usually dressed in fear, sadness, or even shame and insecurity. It was these types of reactions that finally led me to write this book. I want to end the tears by sharing the lessons and principles men and women need to follow in order to build REAL wealth, and not just "look" rich. I want them to be empowered to share these practices with their children and so on, for years to come.

I'm also moved by the people I see in general—those who seem to be chasing money instead of working diligently to amass real wealth—wealth being, in this case, an abundance of assets, investments, and cash; wealth as a measure of net worth, including savings, real estate, and little to no debt. Wealth is what a person has beyond the fancy, expensive clothes and cars we usually see.

"We grow with ownership (home, commercial, etc.) and expand legacy with equity, which means financial access. Used when you want to open a door. All the income you create and cash-flow you manage doesn't have to die with you...the ownership and equity impact can live on for generations; the philosophy... if we can own it, teach it, and own financial products to get us to that place. Who can teach us that financial literacy is just a baby step; that insurance is to protect the wealth we already have, and that buying is not power?"

Pamela Jolly – CAAFP Conference Speech.

This book is an introduction to the work I do for clients. Outside of these pages, I work to educate people on the following:

- their relationship with money and how to thoughtfully distribute it for growth
- how to segment their dollars for specific objectives
- why it's important to practice solid financial principles and teach them to our children via demonstration and conversation.

I also work with clients to understand and become educated on the importance of protecting their wealth through trusts, Last Will and Testaments, Living Wills, legal tax breaks, and from any one generation being able to squander it away. It is the core of what I do. I hope you find this book to be a great start to building a solid financial future (now and beyond) for you and your family.

W
R

CHAPTER TWO

Filling the Knowledge Gaps

"Most people do not plan to fail; they fail to plan."
John Beckley

What did you learn about money management? Were you taught directly, with intention, or were you like the majority of us who picked up our beliefs about money through observation and hard-won experience? Regardless of how you gained your current level of financial knowledge, whether on your own (which was probably not ideal) or if you had someone you trust sit you down for a good talking to, there is still much to learn.

"Recognizing that our financial habits make sense, given our history and the beliefs we internalized about money, allows us to reflect on our financial mistakes with compassion and grace. Understanding that our pasts have a profound impact on our relationship with money sets the stage for our transformation."

Psychology Today, Brad Klontz, Psy.D, CFP
Mind over Money – The Big Lie about Personal Finance

Now, while it is a strong belief that we must look at our situation with compassion and grace, let's now face the hard fact that action is necessary. We cannot continue to overspend and fail to save money. I trust that you know you should be saving for the future and not spending more than you earn, but are you actually doing that? I hope to inspire a transformational change in how you work with your finances. Let's begin with a few questions about your perceptions surrounding money. This is an exercise that I'm asking you to complete inside your book. Don't just think about your answers; write them down.

1) Are you:
    a) impulsive
    b) cautious
    c) competitive
    d) generous
    e) a show-off
    f) a miser
    g) a warrior
2) What messages did your parents convey to you about money when you were growing up?
3) Was money discussed openly in your family?
4) Was it impolite to discuss money in your family?
5) Do you remember who handled the money in your family—your father or mother or both? Do you know or understand why?
6) Did you have less money than your peers growing up?
7) Did your family have enough money to buy everything you wanted?
8) If your parents said no to one of your desires, was it because of money?
9) In your family, did you associate money with rewards?
10) Did you associate money with arguments in your family?

The answers to these questions should begin to give you a glimpse of your past with money and how your money blueprint was created.

Lastly, ask and answer the following, what's one subtle change you can make today that will benefit you, your family, now and in the future?

____

____

____

Take a moment to reflect on your last answer. Inhale while you envision all the possibilities. Then, exhale and continue reading.

If your mindset and habits are congruent and have proven to produce self-sufficiency, contributions to your community, and a life where you can at least depend on more than the basics, I salute you. You are well on your way toward building wealth. However, if you are consistently spending more than you make, impulsively spending over what you've itemized, and failing to see that these thought processes and behaviors are self-destructive to you financially, then we have some work to do.

We're going to start with a reminder: You are NOT and DO NOT HAVE TO BE a social norm. You are a human being who can CHOOSE not to perform the behavioral mishaps of the majority. The power of choice is one of the greatest powers ever given to humans. And in your financial life, you have the power to first assess who you are, where you stand financially, what money means to you, and if you choose to control YOUR BEHAVIOR with MONEY in order to directly benefit you and your community.

I'll conclude this chapter by saying, while it is important to look back on your past relationship with money, be assured that your past only serves as a lesson. Your past does not dictate your future decisions. YOU have the power to choose differently. There is hope for anyone seeking effective change. Keep in mind that decisions made in the now, coupled with information and education—in the form of advisement, coaching, and accountability—can help you create lasting change, and that's what we're going to do.

CHAPTER THREE

Separating Fact from Fiction

"If you were born poor, it is not your fault,
but if you die poor, it is your mistake."
Bill Gates

One of my mentors asked a question to the group he was coaching, "If everything that you believe to be true turned out to be a lie, how would you feel? What would you do?"

Now just ponder upon that for a moment. What beliefs do you hold about money right now that, when you look below the surface, aren't serving/benefiting you? How many of them are actually holding you back from living the life of your dreams? If everything you believe, have been taught, or learned through certain media outlets about finance was proven to be a lie, how shattering would it be to your core belief system?

The next question my mentor asked was, "How could you replace that belief (if it were a lie) with a belief that can serve you?"

In other words, once you learn which of the assumptions you have made or beliefs you hold are false, with what are you going to replace them? Here are a few questions to help you analyze these concepts:

1. What financial beliefs, lessons, and/or behaviors are currently not serving you?

____

____

2. What do you believe about developing a sustainable spending plan (budget)?

____

____

3. What are your thoughts about the use of credit in your personal and business life?

____

____

4. Do you believe that you don't have a lot of money available for savings?

____

____

5. Do you believe you can and should invest a percentage of your net income (take-home income) while still making sure all the bills are paid?

____

____

6. Do you believe that financial planning isn't for the "average" person with an average income?

____

____

7. Do you think saving and investing are reserved only for the wealthy?

____

____

Look through your answers and see if any of them feed into the following myths:

- A budget is restrictive. Following a budget means I can't buy things I want.

- Money is designed for me to enjoy today and not worry about my future. Why save if I can't take it with me?

- Investing ONLY in real estate or stocks or in my business will net me a sufficient nest egg for my future.

- Having a credit card is a sign of wealth. Having a Platinum Black means I'm "ballin".

Let me break it down for you… Letting any of these myths dictate how you use your money will get you into trouble. You'll find yourself buying the $300 handbag but not having $300 cash in it, your checking account, or savings. Or worse, you purchase the bag or anything equivalent and not spend $30-$300 on a disability income or life insurance policy. Yet, you aren't able to work or prematurely pass, leaving you and/or your loved ones with no way to support yourselves because your focus was on "looking" good, not stability and legacy. **Living by any of these myths is a sure way to end up with unmanageable debt and a false sense of financial security.**

"Debt doesn't discriminate. It will come looking for anyone with an empty bank account and a worthy emergency. You already know debt is the enemy. So, suit up."
Author Unknown

W
R

CHAPTER
FOUR
And the Truth Shall Set You Free

"An investment in knowledge pays the best interest."
Benjamin Franklin

Our behaviors develop positively or negatively into habits. Interestingly, those are followed by what we believe about ourselves and the purpose money serves in our lives. For this exercise, I want you to write down the answers to these questions:

1. What is the purpose of money in general?

____

2. What is the purpose of money in your life, specifically?

____

3. Do YOU control the use of YOUR money?

____

4. Do the marketing experts and retailers control your mind and your use of YOUR money OR do YOU?

____

If your answers resemble the following:

1. To buy things…
2. To use on the things I want to…
3. Yes, I control it. I go shopping with it and control the types of red bottoms, sneakers, latest name-brand suits, cars, dresses, etc. I purchase…
4. No, but I do stay tuned in to buy myself or my children the latest games, toys, shoes, etc…

We have work to do, but trust me, that's ok IF you have a commitment to CHANGE IT!

Listen… Our money is ONLY an instrument of exchange to make transactions possible. It is a vehicle that allows us to drive toward the type of lifestyle we desire today, and in the future.

Tony Robbins said, *"If all the money in the world were collected and then distributed evenly to every person in the world, it would end up back in the hands of the ones who were originally wealthy."* **His statement tells us that some people view money as something to be had, while others view money as something to be spent.**

So, are you a spender or an accumulator of money? Is money merely a piece of paper you spend to get the "things you want", or is it a powerful tool you use to provide yourself with power, influence, and/or the lifestyle you dream about?

If your view of money is the latter, yet you're struggling with sticking to a budget or building your savings, then you'll need to take control of your mindset around money. Just ask yourself, "Which mindset better serves and benefits me? And which will make me FEEL better both now and tomorrow?"

Let me tell you about two of my clients; one was a single woman, and the other was married with children. Both women took an honest look at their hard-core spending habits and decided to make significant changes. They realized that their behaviors weren't serving their health or helping with their creation of wealth.

The first client is a bright young lady on the track to massive, professional success. She's stylish, articulate, and mentally sharp. Yet, when we completed just one of the above questionnaires, she uncovered that she was spending approximately $600/month on food ALONE. Mind you, she's single, so this amount was unusually high, she confessed.

In retrospect, she had to admit that she'd much rather have had at least $3,600 ($300 saved over 12 months) to take care of the car transmission that needed repairs; fix the water heater in her home that suddenly spilled water everywhere; or spend towards the international vacation she's desired and still desires today. Instead, she'd been, in her own words, "eating and shitting" her money away. This was a pretty accurate, if not blunt, way to acknowledge that she'd been spending money on something that did not move her any closer to her goals.

The other client I want to tell you about is part of a family of five, who spent just shy of $1,000/month on food. After discussing her and her husband's goals and desires, we noted that they wanted to buy a home, give their children either an education fund or a "getting a start in life" fund and begin their retirement savings. However, there was still significant work to be done if they were to see their goals materialize.

We initially looked at just their food budget. They saw where a decent amount could be saved if they cut down on dining out and applied some cost-curbing behaviors, such as using coupons when they bought groceries, as well as meal planning. The money they saved could then be directed toward investing in their children's futures, etc. They found an agreeable way to serve both their human desire to build memories around eat/dining out and their desire to contribute and invest in their children.

Just as those two clients were able to turn things around, so can you. In the next chapter, I will share with you eight basic principles you can apply to your situation right now—which will help you put your $50K or $250K annual income to work, so you may create TRUE wealth.

CHAPTER FIVE

When You Know Better, You Do Better

"A budget is more than just a series of numbers on a page; it is an embodiment of our values."
Barack Obama

Just like the two clients I mentioned in the previous chapter, you should now have a clearer understanding of what behaviors you need to change in order to better utilize your money. This will serve as a means of moving you toward the lifestyle you ultimately desire. Now, let's focus on what habits you need to cultivate for wealth building.

What follows are Eight Fundamental Principles for Money Management you'll want to incorporate into your life moving forward. These principles aren't anything you haven't heard before; however, more than likely, if you're reading this book, they are new in terms of "making them habits". To ingrain them into your everyday life, you'll want to read them again and again; meditate on them for at least five minutes a day, twenty-one days straight. In doing so, they'll become second nature, and you'll be able to do them without a second thought.

Principle 1: Live Life Abundantly

There is a man I admire greatly. He compels us to live our lives and live them abundantly. Therefore, when you think of minimizing financial waste, don't think about it in terms of what you CAN'T do. Reframe your thinking to understand that His idea of abundance first begins with an intimate, spiritual relationship with Him, and THEN all else is POSSIBLE. Pursue a happy family life, work life, community contributions, and even wealth.

Oh, yes! I believe in a higher power, and I believe He desires us to live an abundant life and lifestyle. Let me just introduce you; His name is "I AM". I AM is anything you need Him to be. In this context, I AM is also known as, Yhwh-Yireh—"The Lord Will Provide". In my opinion, He provides a life plan and fulfillment from the inside-out. He also speaks a lot about money in His book (the Bible). He's raised several kings, men, and women who lived in times of plenty and times of famine. One thing I believe is certain... He never mentioned money or the process of acquiring money to be the number one priority. However, money was spoken of more often than "salvation". See Matthew 25:14-30.

Principle 2: Begin with the End in Mind

This principle requires you to slow down and visualize the future lifestyle you're working for OR the lifestyle you want to live. The easiest way to do this is to look at family members, colleagues, or friends. Who among them are retired and living a lifestyle you desire to live at their age? Which ones are still working?

Of those who are still putting in time on a regular job or business, casually ask them why they're still devoting hours, and in some cases, countless hours working, without any sign of slowing down. Pay attention to who is working because they HAVE to, in order to pay the bills, and who is working because they WANT to and don't need the money to survive. Yet, they have the desire to continue building, creating, and impacting lives and industries.

Those who have saved, spent wisely, and invested find themselves able to do things they enjoy—things they find mentally stimulating. They have the time to volunteer, travel extensively, and play golf or tennis at their leisure. In other words, they are truly living, not just existing from pay day to pay day. For those around you who are in this group, ask them how they were able to get to this point. What steps did they take that led to leaving their businesses or corporate positions? Did they meet with a financial advisor, wealth consultant, or financial coach? If so, how often? What did they discuss? What principles resonated with them in such a way that they followed suit and decided to implement the plan? And finally, why? You may want to listen closely to their answers, as I'm sure you'll find more than one of my principles at the core of their answers.

Now, as you begin to form your future lifestyle image in your mind, understand that it's sometimes easy to envision how you want it to look. Other times, it can be challenging. So it's ok to first gain clarity on what you DO NOT WANT or how it shouldn't look. Then you can create and suitably fixate on what it is YOU DO WANT! Just remember, you want to ultimately create a lifestyle similar to or better than your current lifestyle 20yrs+ from now, and even in your retirement years. Use your current monthly income, bills, and expenses as a vision launch pad. Ask yourself about what activities and places you and your family enjoy now. Take those answers and use them to project into the future the types of lifestyles you want to be able to afford.

Principle 3: Be Financially Aware

Be aware of your gross income (income before taxes are taken), net income (income you take home after "Uncle Sam" gets his cut), and earning potential (income you can earn with a part-time job/business, if you earn another degree or credential, move up the corporate ladder, or scale your business revenue). It is important to realize that your potential to earn income/revenue if you are a business owner is massive over the course of your entire life span compared to if you ONLY work for a W-2 your entire life.

For example, imagine a huge tank holding the $5 million you will earn from the time you were a pimpled-face teenager working at some fast food restaurant, to the time you are gray and decide you no longer want to or need to work. The issue is that none of us receive that $5 million in a lump sum, up front, or as a sign-on bonus to the workforce. Typically, we receive it in the form of monthly income for the work done or the results we created. How you treat, track, save, and spend each one of those dollars MATTERS!

Be aware of taxes. Get clear on what is your "tax bracket". How much of your W-2 income (in the form of taxes you pay) goes to the government annually? What is the appropriate number of withholdings you need to claim on your W-4 that allows you to maintain as much of your money as possible throughout the year, breakeven, pay as little, or receive as little back when you file taxes by April? How much can you legally write-off in business taxes, with either your part-time or full-time business? Make sure to manage and maximize tax deductions. Seek advice and really pay attention to your CPA/Accountant. Be aware of all of your expenses. You created them; therefore, you MUST take responsibility for them—particularly those that are fixed, recurring, AND automatically drafted. Become intimately acquainted with the due dates, amounts owed, and then put a plan in place to reduce or remove unnecessary expenses as possible. This is your "Sustained Spending Plan". Write this plan down somewhere you can refer back to it easily and FREQUENTLY (2+ times per month). You can request a Sustained Spending Plan (budget) proprietary excel spreadsheet by emailing adavis@premeirsolutionsintl.com and scheduling a FREE 20min financial consultation. You'll want to spend about ten minutes each week, and once at the end of the month, going over and updating this plan, and then setting up your spending plan for the next month. As you look it over, ask yourself, "Am I winning financially, or am I wasting money unnecessarily?"

If the answer is, "No, I'm wasting my money," then you know you need to make adjustments in order to assure you come out ahead. If you need help, seek out a financial coach or coaching program (email adavis@premiersolutionsintl.com for details), not just an advisor.

Principle 4: Be Intentional and Take Action

The act of being philosophically deliberate is a quality of our mental state. To give this more meaning, being deliberate in our thoughts, beliefs, desires, and hopes is being consistent in directing our thoughts toward some goal or objective. How do we intend to accomplish an objective without first having a clear and concise course of action?

In addition to your monthly Sustained Spending Plan, you need something that encompasses your mid-term and long-term financial goals. This plan will assist you in successfully reaching a specific financial objective. Think of this purpose as the "bull's-eye" on a dart board. The surrounding circles are also goals for which you are aiming. You can also view the larger circles as more immediate goals that are leading and directing you toward your big ticket item goal and/or retirement.

A majority of people in the world must wisely use their earned income because they were not gifted with an inheritance. This means that they must have a specific intent or aim their earned dollars in a particular direction. These include housing, furniture, food, transportation, utilities, insurances (help us manage our risks against catastrophic issues that can happen in life), amenities that provide a certain quality of life, hobbies, and entertainment that add to the memories of our lives. **Where we often get lost is in our consumption and the world of consumerism.**

For instance, when we are purchasing the latest and greatest iPhone 10, when models 9 and 8 still work just fine, instead of maintaining, saving or investing, we cause an unconscious pattern to develop in other spending areas of our lives. That pattern then becomes a habit, and that habit produces poor results or delays goal achievement. We need to slow down for just a moment prior to spending in order to account for and direct our income toward what we truly desire; after all, a majority of us weren't given a bottomless trust fund.

It will serve you well if you spent money on what is durable, reliable, classic, quality, and dependable, with a sprinkle of trend. Keep in mind, these are items you'll use over the course of the years; if taken care of, they'll last, and you can direct what you save from continuous spending in retail shops to your goals (house, education, 3-12 months savings, and/or real estate property). When you manage the threat of consumption (monetarily and materialistically), you can intentionally ensure you have goals that are accomplished and a cushion, both in your present and future life.

Principle 5: Be Disciplined

The idea of discipline is an elusive thought or principle. At its core, we are speaking about the practice of training yourself to follow a code of behavior. We must realize discipline is a practice engaged each and every day. We NEVER fully arrive. So, the idea of being financially disciplined is a great idea; however, let us make it a flexible principle. It's one where once you've developed your Sustainable Spending Plan, you live by it or operate by it MORE OFTEN THAN NOT!

In this same line of thought, we need to be mindful of our emotional push to spend and when that emotion is being exploited. Ladies, the stress at work, for example, may cause you to desire to visit your favorite mall and splurge. Men, the pressure at work may cause you to visit and spend way too much time and resources at your local bar during Happy Hour. Saying to yourself, "I've worked hard, so I deserve this treat," may be true and well deserved. However, I want to caution you and suggest you slow down, grab a drink (non-alcoholic or other, if drunk responsibly), and evaluate the following: a.) Have you paid yourself? b.) Have you already set aside funds for your discretionary expenses, such as your love and desire to travel? c.) Is, and will, your bank account (NOT CREDIT CARD) still be in a healthy state once you've purchased the item? d.) Would it be better spent in your savings account, so you can purchase the home of your dreams or reduce the amount of time you're in debt. That line of questioning will serve you well before you fall prey to the thought of "I deserve; therefore, I do and spend," and NEVER REACH what you said was important to you.

Lastly, in regards to being disciplined, be real and truthful with yourself when it comes to correctly labeling a want versus what is truly a need. Use this formula to help:
WANT- HAVE = NEED.

Some may say this is a limiting belief; JUST EARN MORE! I agree we should seek and act on ways to increase income with vigor. However, some are trying to make ends meet, and that's their current reality. How many of you know someone whose basic life necessities and responsibilities are not being handled properly? Bills are late, late fees added, accounts overdrawn, credit cards maxed, and money borrowed because they have mismanaged their own, etc. On the contrary, others may already have sufficient income, be financially stable, managing their funds well, and focused on multiplying their investments. This basic principle still stands to serve us all. Therefore, take care of what is needed and what you, through your signature, have agreed to be responsible for—initially as a way to honor those commitments, and then as a way to recognize that just about everything else is a desire that simply adds to the enjoyment, ease, or luxury of life.

Your desires are fine. I just want to caution you again about the importance of ensuring that beyond your responsibilities, you stay firm in saving and investing twenty percent of your net income into your future, and hence, remaining disciplined to your true desires!

Principle 6: Develop and Maintain a Savings Habit and Accounts

I've referred to this Principle as "creating a financial floor you cannot fall through". What does that mean exactly? Let's look at it this way – if you lived on the second floor of a condominium, and you unknowingly left the faucet in the tub running, the water would eventually overflow onto the bathroom floor. If you caught it in time and ended up with just a milliliter or so of water on the floor, you could clean it up with a few towels and a mop. You wouldn't have to spend a ton of money on repairs, and you could be fairly confident that the floor hadn't been damaged to the point where the tub would fall through into your downstairs neighbor's living room.

Now let's apply it to a more realistic situation—one to which you can relate. The transmission on your car calls it quits, and you need to replace it or purchase a new car. With a strong savings account (and a plan to continue saving), you could pay to replace the transmission or put a healthy down payment on a car or pay for a cash car without throwing your current way of life into disarray. In other words, the financial commitment needed to fix the situation would be minimal.

An even more extreme situation would be losing your job or business. What would happen if you weren't able to replace your income for three, six, or even twelve months? Having established a lifestyle by which you lived smart –you've reduced expenses, paid down debt, and put away a significant amount of money – you could survive being without a job for a while, without having to worry.

Having a liquid cash reserve (aka a savings account with at least a year's worth of living expenses) is the same as having a floor you can't fall through. But how do you build such a "floor"? Let's delve a bit further.

I used to hear my father speak about saving, and one strategy he taught me was regarding balancing and reconciling my check book (Do you remember seeing those? LOL). He said, "When you have your income, minus each expense you made, and on the ledger, circle how much you have left (or should have left) at the end of the two week period or month. Now, you'll do the same thing the next pay cycle. This allows you to create a type of savings cushion in your checking account that you are allowing to grow."

When following this method (and depending on the amount stored in an operational checking account versus an amount spent), this effort can help you reduce the chances of over-drafting your checking account, which will then assist in eliminating overdraft and/or late payment fees. More progressive than that is that you're leveling up your checking account without earning more.

This type of savings by itself is similar to having a table with just one leg. It will stand upright, but it's not as sturdy as you need it to be. If there's too much weight on any one side, it can topple over.

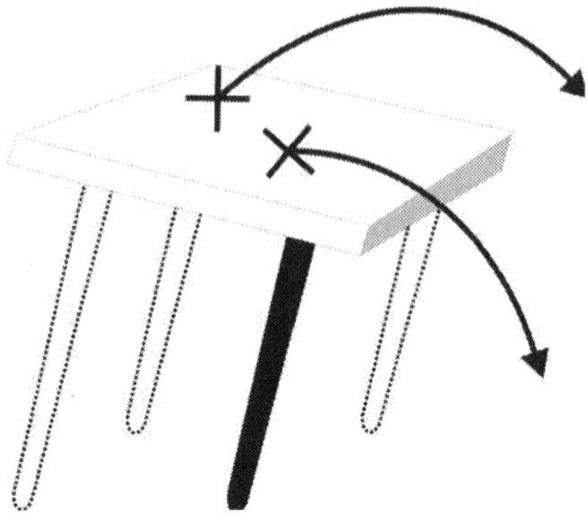

To make this table strong enough to handle a full bounty, you need to add these savings strategies: establish a $1,000 General Emergency Fund, a Lifestyle Emergency Fund (3 to 12 months living expenses), and a 3 to 5 Year Savings Fund for those really BIG expenses, such as a house, motorcycle, or boat. The $1,000 General Emergency Fund is recommended by several of the leading financial gurus in the industry today. This account is for the specific unexpected, however likely, matters that arise. Think of the transmission example I used a few paragraphs back, or worse—your roof was damaged, and you're required to meet your homeowners insurance deductible; you were in an accident, and the insurance company does not expedite or honor your need for a rental car; or a family member out of town or state took ill or died, so you have to take an unexpected trip by yourself or with the entire family. The list could go on and on, but you get the point.

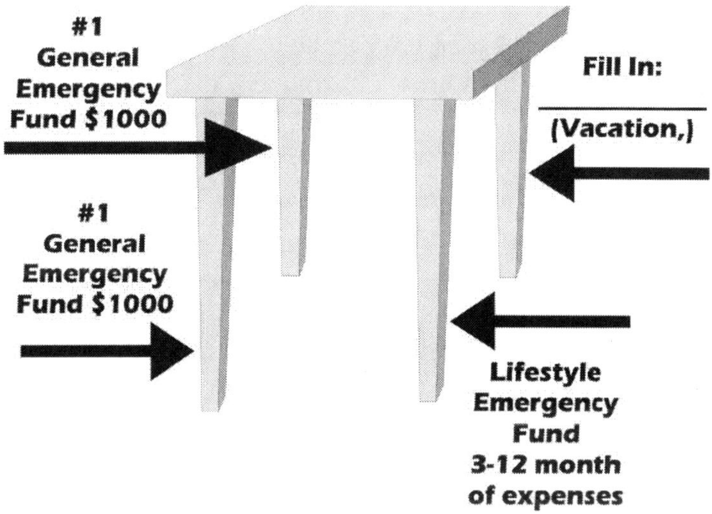

With these types of unexpected, sudden expenses, you DO NOT want to use your immediate cash flow (paycheck) to cover them. If you do, you'll end up throwing off your progress toward a goal or you'll decide to forgo paying a bill(s). Doing so is what the older folks, during my youth, would call, "Robbing Peter to pay Paul".

However catchy the phrase, the bottom line is when you use your paycheck to cover an unexpected expense, and as a result, you cannot meet your everyday fixed expenses, you create a cycle. That cycle looks like that of late payments, extra fees/fines, stress, anxiety, and feeling like you are in the rat race. This has caused many, including myself at one point, to then have to acquire debt that, if not managed properly, is difficult to get out of.

Unforeseen expenses pop up for everyone at some point in time, and in most cases, we are ILL-PREPARED to deal with them financially. However, if we slow down, think through life's potential challenges, and intentionally and systematically set a percentage of our money aside, then we can BE PREPARED to financially handle almost any situation.

Having a Lifestyle Emergency Fund means to set aside enough money that you could meet your current monthly expenses for an extended period of time; a minimum of three months is mandatory, and up to a year's worth is ideal. This strategy is going to take you some time. Be patient and consistent in putting this money away. Your $1,000 Emergency Fund can be the starting point for your Lifestyle Emergency Fund, but as soon as you get a month's worth of expenses above that thousand, separate the two. Keep the $1,000 in one account and continue building your Lifestyle account by itself.

If you want to build this fund faster, consider working extra hours (if you're paid hourly) or beginning a side hustle, be that in the form of a second, part-time gig or your own business. Funnel any additional money earned (found or given) into this account. Ultimately, be patient with your progress. This is not a race; however, the quicker you can accomplish this goal, the better.

And lastly, your long-term goal account is there to cover big events (i.e. weddings, luxury vacations for the family, and/or big investments like a down payment on your dream house). You may be tempted to utilize a credit card for some of them or cover the expense(s) by taking out a loan. Trust me; you want to enjoy whatever the activity is without having to worry about how you're going to pay that high-interest payment each month for the next, however many years. It's much better to be able to meet these expenses with cash payments whenever possible.

What are some ways to fund this account? I'm glad you asked. One of the best ways is to put away the majority of any work bonuses, tax refunds, or other large sums of money you receive above and beyond your paycheck.

With all three of these accounts, you have to develop the habit of automatically, consistently depositing money, and then LEAV-

ING THEM ALONE. Do not make withdrawals casually or for unexpected expenses (house taxes, vehicle purchases, or debt payoffs). You must develop the mindset and decision to let the money sit, grow, and compound—undisturbed until you've reached your saving goal and/or age of retirement, and it's time to withdraw the money to live your dream retirement lifestyle.

I need to also point out something really important when it comes to any retirement accounts you may have, such as your 401(k), Traditional IRA (Individual Retirement Account), and Roth IRA accounts—these are NOT EMERGENCY FUNDS. If they have the word RETIREMENT in the title, or the government has set up parameters for them to be SPECIFICALLY used in your retirement years, lest they penalize you, LEAVE THEM ALONE! Sure, they all have processes you can go through to withdraw money early, but they come with costs. Up front, there are cash penalties, and then you have the added income you are required to claim on your taxes, which could result in you owing a significant amount. Long-term costs are the reduction in the amount of money you now have toward your life when you retire. Your retirement account(s) is just that—money set aside to help fund your lifestyle once you leave the workforce.

Principle 7: Pay Yourself First

Do you believe that putting an extra $50-$5,000 toward a bill is MORE IMPORTANT than having the perspective of putting that same or some equivalent amount toward your savings funds? How about this... Do you believe that treating yourself to the latest pair of shoes, handbag, designer jeans, top, car, etc. is a sign of how much you value yourself? I'm just going to put this out here; the answer to both of these questions is a resounding "NO!"

If you were in need of that $50-$5,000 to help address an emergency situation like those I described before, do you think you could get it back from whichever company you paid it to? It's a safe bet that on most accounts, none of the major corporations you pay money to would grant that request, no matter how dire your situation was. And trust me, going into debt to buy the latest "whatever" is not showing yourself love. The best way to use your hard earned dollars and show how much you truly value yourself is to list your name at the top of the monthly expense list as the first and most important EXPENSE/INVESTMENT. When I say "You", it's as in keeping a percentage of your money in HARD COLD CASH ($50-$100 on hand at all times), putting twenty plus percent (20%) of your income into your savings accounts, as I mentioned in the previous principle, and then individually paying a little more towards your future with an account not associated with your job's qualified plan. Perhaps, that is your personal non-qualified, Traditional or Roth IRA, Annuity, or Cash Value Life Insurance contract.

Is there no additional money for yourself because your car note is more than 5% of your income? Or is it because when you saw that big luxurious house, it just spoke to your soul, and you reasoned that you just had to have it? You have no extra money; however, you have a cable service with over 300 channels of which you only really watch two, ok, maybe three channels, and yet you pay $1,200+/year ($100/month). I'll address these issues in the next principle.

Principle 8: Live on Less than You Make

At what level do you consume your paycheck, commission, or business revenue? Are you living and spending? If that last paragraph described your monthly expense situation, you are living to spend. You need to reduce your spending as much as possible, and as quickly as possible, so you can put the other principles into play.

Can we agree that if you live indoors and have food to eat, clothes to wear, and heat in the winters, you have most of the things you need? If you don't think so, I would venture to say that you struggle to identify what's a need versus a want. Let's explore this further… I understand that the context here is more about shifting from spending on things you really don't need, may not use, and in ways that move you further away from your financial goals, to doing what it takes to reach those goals and live the lifestyle you really want.

Why is living on less more important? What purpose does it serve? In our current society, with American consumerism levels at an alarmingly high rate, the purpose is to help re-establish financial peace of mind, control, and stability with anticipated personal financial wealth accumulation. Thus, if you send out all the income you receive, it becomes self-defeating and counterproductive.

Let's look at a few ways we can live on less. Where have you financially overcommitted? What types of regular, monthly, recurring expenses have you taken the responsibility for payment that block your ability to pay yourself, save for big events/purchases, etc.? Stop for a moment, think through your obligations, and write ONLY the expenses that don't allow you to be financially responsible and stable.

EXPENSE: ____________________ COST: ____________________

EXPENSE: ____________________ COST: ____________________

EXPENSE: ____________________ COST: ____________________

EXPENSE: ____________________ COST: ____________________

EXPENSE: ____________________ COST: ____________________

EXPENSE: ____________________ COST: ____________________

Now, list the upcoming financial commitments you have that aren't monthly. These expenses are future, one-time payments you're planning, such as a vacation, your wedding, or the participation in or attendance of a wedding, where you have to travel quite a distance from home. You may also be planning automobile upgrades, like updating the sound system or getting a new paint job; maybe you've decided to buy a snowmobile, get a tattoo(s), or purchase season tickets to see your favorite sports team or theater company.

Which of those types of financial commitments have you already made or have coming up this year?

EXPENSE: ________________ COST: ________________

EXPENSE: ________________ COST: ________________

EXPENSE: ________________ COST: ________________

EXPENSE: ________________ COST: ________________

EXPENSE: ________________ COST: ________________

EXPENSE: ________________ COST: ________________

If you're not one paycheck away from your dominoes falling, and if you have your savings and investments in place, then these things should rightly be a part of your lifestyle for enjoyment. However, if your "financial table" is missing a leg or two, or sadly, the table top sits totally on the floor, then you have a lot of work to do before you can comfortably spring for those big, future expenses. Nonetheless, there's hope.

Looking at these two aforementioned lists, does it serve you to continue the monthly obligations or move forward with the one-time big purchases this year? Be completely honest with yourself. If your savings accounts aren't fully funded, if you are behind on any or all of your bills, or if you'd have to borrow money in order to pay for that one, big expense, then NO; it does not serve you to move forward with those big, one-time expenses.

"No" is a very powerful word, yet "Not Right Now" is a powerful phrase to keep in mind; in this case, it's placing a TEMPORARY hold on the big purchases you want to make. Until you've put all four legs on your financial table, so that it's stable and strong enough to withstand most of life's surprises, you need to cut back on all things "luxury". Cancel subscriptions, get rid of cable, moderate your dining out, design an enjoyable and memorable STAYCATION, and tell your friend who is getting married that now is not the best time, and then find them a nice gift (they will be happy to pay to feed one to four less mouths at the reception I'm sure…LOL). Do whatever you can at this point to curb big spending on one or two items, and instead, invest in activities and habits that will net you big returns.

W
R

CHAPTER SIX

Dumping the Debt

"Some debts are fun when you are acquiring them, but none are fun when you set about retiring them."
Ogden Nash

Most people are carrying some sort of debt—from credit cards, to student loans, to the mortgage on their dream house. Somehow, in some way, almost everyone you know owes money. Depending on your age, current retirement account values, and the amount of debt you have, why might you consider it important to reduce, if not outright eliminate your debt? I'll tell you. The time value of money for a 40-year-old versus a 20-year-old is drastically different. In other words, the 20-year-old has a lot of time ahead of them to work and earn money, pay off debt, and invest for growth purposes.

Factor in the wonder of compound interest where money is working for you (being multiplied to your investment amount) versus interest working against you in the form of credit card type interest where you're paying interest back to a financial institution, and in many cases, high interest rates. See, the 20-year-old theoretically stands to make more from saving in investment accounts over the long run of TIME than someone, say my age of 40+. So, it is important to acquire little debt, pay any charge in full at the end of each month (when possible), and/or apply other useful debt elimination strategies, WHILE saving AS MUCH AS POSSIBLE in accounts where your money is accumulating (growing) and multiplied.

A 40-year-old, on the other hand, has maybe 20-25 working years left for him/her to work, earn, save, and invest in a focused manner. Not to mention, that 40-year-old more than likely has quite a bit more for which they're financially responsible. It's paramount that the older you are, the more you need to be efficiently and effectively saving, investing, and managing debt, while accomplishing your other financial goals. Therefore, my recommendation for this age group is to aggressively manage and pay down debt, but DO NOT DUMP debt when your investment accounts do NOT HAVE ENOUGH TIME to grow and multiply.

My suggestion is to minimize ACQUIRING ANY ADDITIONAL, FRIVOLOUS DEBT, instead STARTING NOW, and do what you can to eliminate the personal loan, credit card, and vehicle debt you currently have. The goal is to set your future lifestyle up similar to your current. And realize you also must show yourself and this society we live in that you know how to manage money and debt.

Let me introduce to you the theory of "Ground Zero". The theory of Ground Zero is simple and can be explained in the diagram below. There are the debtors, savers, and wealth accumulators. Each category starts on the same line called, Ground Zero. Yet the each operate fundamentally different. See the debtor has the mindset to borrow and use other people's money for one reason or another. You use their money, which puts you in someone's debt (owing an institution) and are then charged more for the use of "THEIR MONEY". Many pay as little as possible ("the minimum due") each month. And then we see or want something else shiny OR an expected major expense beyond our cashflow ability occurs (i.e. transmission blows), and we use the card again or open another.

So we start at ground zero—not having the money ourselves—and we consistently work our way back to ground zero, which represents paying off the loans. The saver has a mindset to save more consistently than not. Yet, when an unexpected event occurs, s/he self-finances the expense with his/her dollars and end back down at ground zero. Now, the wealth accumulator has the mindset to save and invest in accounts that safe, certain accounts have a return rate of 1.5% - 5%, and aren't penalized nor taxed on those dollars. Also, s/he opens and funds accounts that provide a potentially higher return of 6%+ and/or real estate where passive income (rental income) is generated. And s/he has the funds available, if needed, to fund a project, and savings if an unexpected life or business expense requires, it; YET, s/he DOES NOT INTERRUPT ANY ACCOUNT THAT COMPOUNDS.

THEORY OF GROUND ZERO:

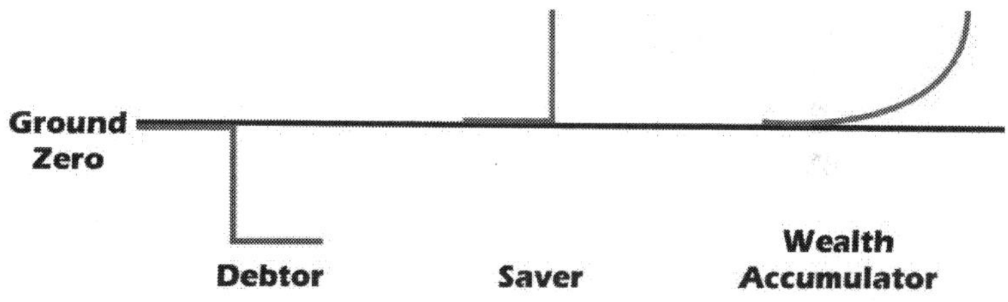

For some of us who aren't aware, it's important to explore what your "credit score" is and how it is determined. Your credit score is a three-digit number generated by a mathematical algorithm, which is produced by using information in your credit report. It's designed to predict risk, specifically, the likelihood that you will become seriously delinquent on your credit obligations in the 24 months after scoring.

Your credit score can mean the difference between being denied or approved for credit. It also determines the interest rate you'll pay over the life of a loan. A good score can help you qualify for an apartment rental and even help you get utilities connected without a deposit.

There is a multitude of credit scoring models in existence, but there's one that dominates the market—the FICO credit score. According to MyFICO.com, the consumer website for the FICO score developer, "90 percent of all financial institutions in the U.S. use FICO scores in their decision-making process." FICO scores range from 300 to 850, where a higher number indicates lower risk. A consumer has three FICO scores, one for each credit report provided by the three major credit bureaus: Equifax, Experian, and TransUnion. Unfortunately, consumers currently have access to only their Equifax and TransUnion FICO scores. Experian ended its agreement with MyFICO.com in 2009.

Source: myFICO.com

Your score is determined by the information entered into your credit report. Data on your credit report is categorized into five major sections. A scoring algorithm takes this data and ranks it—some categories count more heavily than others, so the ranking in that category will have a more significant effect on your overall score. The five categories are as follows:

- Payment history: (35 percent)—your account payment information, including any delinquencies and public records.
- Amounts owed: (30 percent)—how much you owe on your accounts. The amount of available credit you're using on revolving accounts is heavily weighted.
- Length of credit history: (15 percent)—how long ago you opened accounts and the time since account
- activity.
- Types of credit used: (10 percent)—the mix of accounts you have, such as revolving and installment.

My Fico Chart

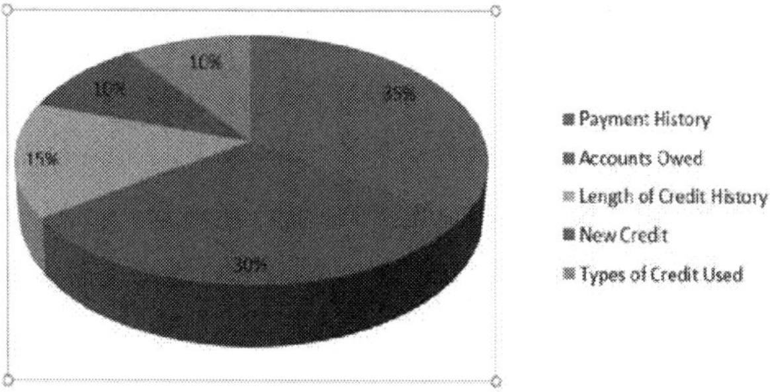

- New credit: (10 percent)—your pursuit of new credit, including credit inquiries and the number of recently opened accounts.

Within a scoring model, there's more than one formula used to calculate a score, and each formula is designed for a category of consumers with similar credit profiles. The information in your credit report determines which formula is used. If you are new to credit, for instance, the scoring model will put you into a category for people with young credit histories, and use a scoring formula specific to that group. Such groups are called, "scorecards". Within that group, recent inquiries may cost more points than they would for a different group.

Getting a copy of your credit report is fairly easy, while getting your actual credit score, however, is not. Federal law mandates the consumer's right to a free, annual credit report from each credit reporting agency, but not to a free credit score. There are, nonetheless, plenty of online sites that will provide you with close approximations of your score for little to no fees.

Now that you are more educated on what credit is made up of, let's discuss strategies to get you out of debt.

Debt Strategy #1: Debt Snowball Method

Do you remember building snowballs in the backyard as a kid? You probably learned that the fastest way to build a snowball was to pack some snow into a tight ball, and then start rolling it through the yard. As it gained momentum, the snowball grew into something more like a snow boulder. It was a good technique for building snowballs as a kid, and it's an even better method for paying off your non-mortgage debt.

The Debt Snowball Method is a debt reduction strategy where you pay off debts in order of smallest to largest, gaining momentum as each balance is paid off. When the smallest debt is paid in full, you roll the money you were paying on that debt into the next smallest balance. Dave Ramsey made this methodology popular and describes the process like this:

Step 1: List your debts from smallest to largest.
Step 2: Make minimum payments on all your debts, except the smallest.
Step 3: Pay as much as possible on your smallest debt.
Step 4: Repeat until each debt is paid in full.

Source: https://www.daveramsey.com/blog/how-the-debt-snowball-method-works?ictid=aw15

Debt Strategy #2: Bi-Weekly Payments

I've reprinted an article written by Brian O'Connell. He expertly explains how this strategy is most helpful for paying down one of the largest debts any of us will have —our mortgage.

Why Paying Your Mortgage Twice a Month
Can Save You Serious Money.
By Brian O'Connell
May 17, 2018

Homeowners looking to cut their overall mortgage debt can get the job done by doubling the number of payments they make to their mortgage company every year. The practice is called "bi-weekly mortgage payments", a strategy where mortgage loan customers pay their mortgage loan every two weeks, instead of once a month. The idea is to chop down your mortgage payment more quickly, and in the process, lower the amount of interest you pay on your mortgage overall. (For more on how interest and APRs actually work, read this.)

The numbers support that sentiment. Paying your mortgage every two weeks adds one full payment each year (13 payments—based on 26 bi-weekly payments each year, versus 12 monthly payments).

Savings Add up with Bi-Weekly Payments

Consider a traditional 30-year mortgage of $200,000 with an interest rate of 6.5%. Normally, that would require the homeowner to make a monthly payment of $1,264.14. By using a bi-weekly payment plan, the homeowner would pay $632.07 every two weeks, and, in doing so, s/he would cut six years of payments off the mortgage loan, ultimately saving $58,747 off the total amount of the loan. (Are you looking for help refinancing your mortgage? If so, please read this.) "A bi-weekly payment plan is far more effective than merely sending one additional payment per year," says Michael Hausam, a realtor and mortgage broker in Newport Beach, CA. "Your loan balance accrues interest every day, and reducing that principal balance every 14 days (26 half payments per year) saves more in interest charges than one full additional payment every 12 months, even though the total amount in payments every year remains the same."

Lisa Orban, an author and Illinois-based homeowner, has been a regular bi-weekly mortgage payment payer since she purchased her residence and has a good reason for the strategy.

"I pay bi-weekly for a number of reasons, but the primary one is almost immediately more money is put towards the principal rather than the interest," Orban says. "The payment on the first of the month, more money goes towards interest, but the payment on the 15th shifts, and more money is put towards the mortgage loan principal."

It's important to note, however, that not all mortgage services allow bi-weekly payments. To find out where you stand, reach out to your lender and ask about your bi-weekly mortgage payment options. If they are permitted, your lender can walk you through the process of setting up the new payment plan.

Source: https://www.experian.com/blogs/ask-experian/why-paying-your-mortgage-twice-a-month-can-save-you-serious-money/

Traits of People Who Experience Debt-Free Living

In case you were wondering what you can look forward to when you become debt-free, here are a few positive "side effects" you might enjoy:

1. Being Countercultural

Despite normal convention, these people realize debt isn't a tool. Society tells us that you have to have a credit card to survive; you can't go to college without student loans; and you'll always have a car payment. However, those who are experiencing debt-free living don't buy into these norms. Credit cards aren't necessary for their everyday lives. Car payments don't take a chunk of money from their budgets. They treat debt like leftovers they find at the back of their fridge. Whether it's debt or a week-old meatloaf, they get rid of it! Debt is normal. So be weird!

2. Having and Exercising Self-Control

According to Dave Ramsey, adults make a plan and follow it. Children do what "feels" good. Someone who really wants to get out of debt has the willpower to walk right past the shoe section or the flat-screen TV aisle without making an impulse purchase. They aren't swayed to buy something simply because it's on sale that day. They are wise enough to know that purchasing something isn't going to erase all their problems and make them feel better. Why? They know not to buy those things unless they can pay cash. They are willing to wait, work, and save.

3. Being Confident

A person who believes in their money plan doesn't care what others think of them. They're fine with driving an older car because it doesn't have a payment. They don't need to take expensive vacations just to post a glamorous photo on social media. They actually look at price tags and not only at brand names. Why? They have given up on trying to keep up with the Joneses.

And guess what? This kind of steadfast discipline frees up more money to attack their debts. With each debt they pay off, their confidence grows by leaps and bounds.

4. Being Goal-Driven

That's a no-brainer, right? Debt-free living is a goal, so people who want to accomplish it must keep that objective in front of them. They set goals that are specific, measurable, achievable, relevant, and have an expiration date. They determine what they want to do and map out their strategy to make it happen.

5. Having "Gazelle" Intensity

If you've attended Financial Peace University (Dave Ramsey), you probably remember Dave talking about "Gazelle Intensity". That's when you are so fed up with debt, you run as fast as you can (like a gazelle from a predator) in the opposite direction. This means you work to squeeze every single dollar you can from your budget. You become an expert at couponing, looking for sales at every turn, and even working a side hustle. You are all in to out-running any accumulation of debt.

6. No Longer Being Materialistic

Someone who is materialistic places too much emphasis on "stuff". They borrow up to their eyeballs to pay for their vacation, car, and oversized house. People who are determined to get out of debt know money doesn't buy happiness, so they don't fall into the trap of wanting as much stuff as they can get. They have become content with what they have and aren't seeking to buy their happiness.

7. Being More Willing to Make Sacrifices That Move You Forward

Eating out, going to movies every week, and getting the premium cable package—these are the types of things a person might have to avoid while becoming debt-free. But keep in mind... Budget cuts are just temporary. Once the debt is gone, there is more room in the budget for those dinner-and-a-movie dates.

CHAPTER
SEVEN

Mitigating Risks

"The first step in the risk management process is to acknowledge the reality of risk. Denial is a common tactic that substitutes deliberate ignorance for thoughtful planning."
Charles Tremper

Have you seen or experienced a family member needing in-home or assisted living care? Have you ever suffered an injury, accident, or illness that prevented you from being able to work in your primary job duties? Have you ever had a loved one pass prematurely, and the family is left with not only the funeral expenses, but also the loss of income? The philosophy here is to protect against catastrophic circumstances that can occur to you even if they have not yet happened, since it can be financially devastating.

As a mentor stated it to me, "Protect against the things that can go wrong, so as or when you've finished building your savings and investments, you can protect and enjoy the things that go right."

What types of risk can put you, your family, your finances, and your future at risk? Let's list, provide examples, and then explain with one agreement. The agreement is that you will answer the questions asked, take a moment to review, and then discuss them with a professional financial advisor or insurance agent within that area of risk management, one who has extensive experience in risk-based protection. During your conversation, focus on what your current program design entails, and really listen to whether they ask you quality questions that enlighten you, as well as help to determine if you are adequately protected or woefully under insured.

Let's explore the following:
Homeowners and/or Renters Insurance is a form of property insurance that covers losses and damages to an individual's house and assets in the home. Homeowners insurance also provides liability coverage against accidents in the home or on the property. In plain English, this means that if a tree falls, wind blows your home down, or a fire consumes your home or your neighbor's apartment, and it affects your living conditions, it can now be repaired or rebuilt at the expense of the insurance company, based on your contract and premium payments. Moreover, it also covers you if someone were to sue you, for example, regarding a slip and fall in your home and decide to hold you responsible for repayment of doctors' bills, lost time from work, or just because they see an opportunity to financially "come up" through a frivolous law suit against you.

Typical homeowners' insurance policies offer coverage for damage caused by fires, lightning strikes, windstorms, and hail. However, it's important to know that not all natural disasters are covered by homeowners insurance. For instance, damage caused by earthquakes and floods are not typically covered by homeowners insurance. When closing on your home or refinancing, make sure you speak with your property and casualty insurance agent. This will enable you to NOT only confirm what your mortgage company requires, but also to stay abreast of your policy as time and potential claims occur.

Renters insurance is a form of homeowners insurance, except, because you are renting, it protects your personal belongs and covers some damages to the property in the event of water damages, etc. A single mother of three experienced a house fire, didn't have any renters insurance, and lost it all. Family members established a GoFundMe account, and if it hadn't been for that account, she would not have been able to financially support her family during this time.

Car (auto) Insurance is a contract between you and the insurance company that protects you against financial loss in the event of an accident or theft. In exchange for you paying a premium, the insurance company agrees to pay your losses as outlined in your policy. Instead of paying out of pocket for auto accidents, people pay annual premiums to an auto insurance company; the company then pays all or most of the costs associated with an auto accident or other vehicle damage. A type of auto insurance, referred to as liability insurance, is the part that covers damage that you cause to other drivers during an accident—more specifically, vehicle and property damage. It is a required provision in virtually all auto insurance policies.
We see accidents almost daily as we drive on any major highway. And while some are fatal, others are incidents of just a fender bender. Either way, not having adequate insurance can cause a major dip into your cash flow or savings, and not having any insurance in most states can cause major fines or fees, and on occasion, a short stay in jail. If you cause an accident, make someone's life financially whole again by speaking to your auto insurance agent to determine what that might look like for you and your level of need.

Health Insurance is a type of insurance coverage that pays for medical and surgical expenses incurred by the insured. Health insurance can reimburse the insured for expenses incurred, from illness or injury, or pay the care provider directly. As medical care advances and treatments increase, health care costs also increase. The purpose of health insurance is to help you pay for care. It protects you and your family financially in the event of an unexpected serious illness or injury that could be very expensive.

Disability Insurance, also known by some in the industry as "paycheck protection", is intended to replace some of a working person's income/paycheck when a disability prevents him/her from working. It does not cover medical care or long-term care services. There are two types of disability policies: Short-Term Disability (STD) and Long-Term Disability (LTD). STD policies have a waiting period of zero to 14 days, with a maximum benefit period of no longer than two years.

Life Insurance is a contract between an insurer and a policyholder in which the insurer guarantees payment of a death benefit to named beneficiaries upon the death of the insured. The insurance company promises a death benefit in consideration of the payment of premium by the insured. A lapse in premium payments could result in loss of such benefits.

Long Term Care (LTC) Insurance is another type of insurance. It is coverage that provides nursing-home care, home-health care, and personal or adult day care for individuals above the age of 65 and/or with a chronic or disabling condition that needs constant supervision. LTC insurance offers more flexibility and options than many public assistance programs.

Let me ask you a few questions that are worth thinking about now. More importantly, I want you to write your answers next to each, so you can really think through this important part of life that is often left unplanned.

• Who would you consider capable and willing to care for you?

____

• How would this impact that caregiver's lifestyle?

____

• Have you considered the impact to your lifestyle if a parent (or in-law) became dependent on you for long-term care?

____

• Are you familiar with the approximate costs of long-term care services? ________________________________

While the costs for custodial care services in a nursing home typically range from $100-$300 per day ($3-$9K/month), which is $36K-$108K of annual income. Second, the average cost of care inside one's home is approximately $19-$21/hour. Third, assisted living facilities range on average approximately $3,477/month. Care provided by a family member(s) may not have a direct cost; however, there is an intangible cost. The family member(s) either can no longer work full-time or reduces his/her hours at work.

Can you imagine your life at age 90? Admittedly, even though it's not easy to create the image in your minds, it's worth spending a few minutes to forecast the vision. It's just like with planning and forecasting in our mind's eye to see ourselves reaching our personal, professional, and/or financial goals. It is something that's necessary for this stage of our lives. Otherwise, the reality and quality of our lives can look and feel different than we would want. My grandfather is now 90 years young, and he lives in his home while being cared for by his second oldest daughter, who does an amazing job to ensure his good health and well-being. He is blessed to be living a long, rich life and receiving quality care.

The point being made in the previous paragraph is that, unfortunately, this was NOT by design, rather by default. While my aunt is happy to care for him, her life looks drastically different from what it might otherwise, based on the conversations I recall having with her concerning her business goals. However, professional custodial care is so expensive that she couldn't be relieved for even a few hours of the day. Think about that for a moment. Now, let's step into our golden years with such intentionality that, not only do we create the life we desire, we can enhance the lives of those whom we love, rely on, and expect to share our future lifestyle with us.

CHAPTER EIGHT

Don't Look Rich, Be Rich

"Rich people have small TVs and big libraries.
And poor people have small libraries and big TVs."
Chris Rock

Wealth is *"Quiet"*
Rich is *"Loud"*
Poor is *"Flashy"*

I see it every day—the young hot-shot or young mogul who LOOKS wealthy. We're constantly being fed images of what "rich" looks like on social media, in magazines, online, or on TV. S/he has a sweet sports or luxury car, nice suit, or chic, casual attire, designer sunglasses, designer watch, and the trendiest, expensive, name-brand shoes.

Why Do People Try to Look Rich?

This is an interesting question, the answer to which takes different shapes. On one hand, the look being displayed has been admired and replicated over the course of the last few decades. Marketers have been working feverishly to convince us that success doesn't come first; the look does. Finance the look, and success will be yours. This sounds silly, but it works perfectly. You know what the truth probably is about the businessman described above:

- Porsche: Financed, by the skin of his credit score. They definitely didn't get a zero interest new car loan!
- Business Suit: Credit card. He only owns one and hates paying to get it dry cleaned.
- Sunglasses: Credit card.
- Designer Watch: Credit card or it could also be a convincing "replica".
- Leather Shoes: Credit card. He had to make a payment to free up enough credit.
- Smartphone: No stock quotes, just excited text messages about the job interview.
- Important Meeting: Job interview. Hopefully, his sharp look will land the job.

On the other hand, the lack perpetuated over the generations stimulates a strong desire to come from the shadows of poverty, second-hand clothes/shoes, and the inner dialogue of wanting more, yet not seeing, feeling, or being able to produce the lifestyle we desire. This is accompanied by the belief that we are worth more, yet not certain how to attain it within our bank and brokerage accounts, along with our real estate portfolios. So, while working our way up from the ashes, like a phoenix, we begin with what seems more attainable. And THAT is the look—whether by our cash flow that flew out the window with these purchases or "debt cards", better known as credit cards.

My deepest desire is that this will not always be the case for my clients and those reading this book, yet statistics show that most people who look successful, will only "look" successful. Can we make an agreement to no longer buy into the image being portrayed? Let us not look at frugality with disgust and disdain. Instead, let's learn to embrace and even celebrate its benefits. A frugal person has decided to place value on items or assets that, while not portrayed in a positive light, serve their greater purpose of...FINANCIAL STABILITY, SECURITY, AND PEACE OF MIND.

Here lies the problem, and internal lesson, we can glean from financing those suits, shoes, sunglasses, and car. Debt or credit interest will eat at your current and future income so terribly that you will have a hard time mentally and practically to rebuild a strong financial future. When you are young and making very little money, spending your hard earned cash on flashy, yet obsolete, items is the absolute worst time to be paying high retail prices and high amounts of interest. Not only are you losing that income to interest expense, but you're losing all the future interest that money would have been earning. Save Money Where You Can Sometimes, it is hard to go against the grain. However, while your friends are putting on airs, not caring, not directing their money towards the goals they say matter most, and paying tons of interest on financed goods, your story and picture will look different. You will look fashionable based on finding great sale items. You will drive nice and reliable vehicles where your car note is no more than five percent (5%) of your net income (take home income). You will find ways to accentuate your looks—haircuts for men, hair and lashes (natural or barter) for women, waxing, etc.; manicures and pedicures will stay on point whether you chose the natural look or decide less than $50/month is sufficient, especially if you have no or very little savings. Instead, you will bank that money first to provide yourself with a savings cushion and then transition it into earning income (i.e. stocks, mutual funds, brokerage accounts, real estate, and long-term future lifestyle savings aka retirement savings). That is a huge step toward financial independence. Years up the road, while your friends are still paying off unrealistic mortgages or credit cards; trying to continue crawling up the corporate ladder and win the rat race; or having garage sales on items that are no longer in style, taking up space, and hold zero long-term value, you'll be able to enjoy your financial independence no matter your income level.

We as people of all races and genders, especially young people, underestimate our money's ability to work for us. Because of this short-sightedness, we do not allow the pennies of interest to grow into dollars of interest. We do not allow those dollars of interest to develop into supplemental paychecks. Moreover, we do not allow those supplemental paychecks to manifest into a main source of income, free from punching someone else's or your own time clock. We see pennies of interest/investment income, say "What's the point," and spend it on the next shiny thing we see.

Here is a great article that really helps bring this very important concept together:

Millionaire State of Mind, Money & Wealth, Motivation
By Marc Hill
May 8, 2017

The goal is to become rich, not to look rich.

Most people never become wealthy because they waste too much money on buying symbols of success that depreciate. They are more focused on looking rich, instead of becoming rich. The rich stay rich because they spend like they are poor. The poor stay poor because they spend like they are rich. Living below your means and investing your extra income is how you build wealth. No matter how much money you make, you must spend less than you earn.

Don't be in such a rush to look successful. Once the average person begins to earn a decent income, the first thing they do is go and buy a new car, designer clothes, and a big house that has more space than they need. Don't fall into the trap of pretending to be rich. A rich person can pretend to be poor forever, but a poor person cannot pretend to be rich for long.

Many people just want attention and popularity, but rich people are primarily focused on the money and freedom. Get rich first, and you can always enjoy the luxury later. It's a sure recipe for long-term success and wealth.

Luxury goods are not going anywhere. Material goods get better every year. Buy assets that produce income, and take that money and purchase more income producing assets. Repeat this process, and you will eventually become rich. Dividend paying stocks from great companies and rental property in prime locations are great examples of assets that produce income.

Think about buying car companies' stock instead of buying a new car. Buy ownership shares in the beer company instead of just drinking the beer. It's better to own shares in the shoe company instead of having a massive shoe collection. Think like an owner, not a consumer.

After you become rich, then you can buy all the material goods you want with no consequences to your financial security. Wait until you are TRULY rich. New homes get better every year. Luxury cars get better every year. Designer clothes and fancy watches look nicer every year. Smartphone models are replaced with bigger and more advanced ones every year.

You can always buy that later.

The interesting thing is that the wealthier I become, the less I desire material goods. You don't have anything to prove when you really have money. Word spreads fast when you are truly rich because people see the lifestyle you live and the time freedom you enjoy. Most people who are truly rich don't flaunt their wealth because they don't want to attract freeloaders, thieves, and beggars.

The essence of being rich is to have options. Wealth affords you the option to live where you want, spend the time you want, enjoy as much time with family as you want, help the poor, impact the world, etc. Luxury goods are not the essence of being wealthy. The novelty wears off from material goods after three to six months.

Have you ever seen a new car that you loved, and a year later, it didn't look so great anymore? Have you ever bought new clothes or jewelry, and a month later, you didn't really like it as much? Your legacy won't be about the things you possessed. Nobody really cares about the material possessions of Warren Buffet, Bill Gates, and other wealthy people. Nobody will care about how nice of a car, clothes, or home you had. You will be known for the impact you had on others and the legacy of wealth you left behind.

Psalms 13:22 says, *"A righteous man leaves back an inheritance for his children's children."* Don't lose your opportunity to really be rich by trying to look rich through materialism. According to Luke 12:15, *"One's life does not consist in the abundance of his possessions."* The goal is to be rich, not look rich. You can buy nice things, but get rich first.

CHAPTER NINE

It's Never Too Late

"When money realizes that it is in good hands,
it wants to stay and multiply in those hands."
Idowu Koyenikan

Jeff Rose, Forbes Contributor, wrote an amazing article that summed up many of my thoughts quickly and concisely. Here is the meat of the article that I want to share (to read the article in its entirety use the following link):

https://www.forbes.com/sites/jrose/2015/09/30/ways-to-build-wealth-fast-that-your-financial-advisor-wont-tell-you/#4a555fce6641

"9 Ways to Build Wealth Fast
(That Your Financial Advisor Might Not Tell You)"
Jeff Rose
Sep. 30, 2015

…I know, this isn't very exciting, but this is the definition of wealth. As Todd Tresidder of FinancialMentor.com says, "Great wealth builders focus on both saving money and earning more."

What Todd is pointing to here is the gap between your expenses and your income. Expenses should always be lower than your income. The larger that gap, the more wealth you can accumulate.

Let's face it; you can't invest unless you have money to invest. If you're currently living beyond your means and have no additional money to put to work for you, you'll never build wealth. So where do you go from here?

1. Save on Vehicles

I was fortunate enough to have learned this lesson when I was still in college. This led to me driving a 1998 Chevy Lumina that was completely paid for because I inherited it from my deceased grandmother. Not having a car payment allowed me to invest into myself, my Roth IRA, and my 401(k).

According to Jason Fogelson for Forbes: "The biggest mistake a car buyer can make, especially in the age of the internet, is to buy a car without doing research first. Some buyers are so eager to get through the car-buying process that they don't take the time to find out everything they can about vehicle reliability, pricing and financing."

I agree, completely. But let's focus on the financing part for a minute. Car loans come with ridiculous interest rates that nobody should have to pay to obtain transportation. Car loans can easily be one of the highest-cost debts of many American households.

Too many people view the car payment as "normal". Sure, it's normal, but "normal" won't help you produce wealth, my friend. Instead, consider doing what I did and drive a car that you own outright. It'll be easier on your pocketbook over the long-term – I promise.

2. Save on Shelter

In addition to that, my wife and I rented a house for the first year that we were together. Not having the mortgage payment allowed us to build up our emergency fund and also save for our retirement.

But what if renting seems to be more expensive than having a mortgage payment? According to Beth Braverman for Forbes: "Rentals offer far more flexibility. Buying a home typically means committing to a 30-year mortgage. Most people don't stay in a home for anywhere near that amount of time, but it's much harder to pick up and move from a home you own than it is to leave a rental."

And what happens when you can't sell your home when you need to move due to a job change or another reason? You pay a whole lot of money not only for the house you can't sell, but also for the house you move into.

If you need flexibility, consider renting like we did – even if the rent payment is higher than a comparable home with a mortgage payment.

3. Don't Buy Crap

Lastly, we didn't buy crap we didn't need.

Ask yourself what you really need and really don't need. Do you really need that million-inch flat screen TV? No, you don't!

4. Save a Percentage of Your Income

Savers like my wife and I are definitely in the minority. Very few people save a substantial amount for the future, but if you think we're in the minority, then check out Pete from MrMoneyMustache.com who advocates that you should be saving between 30 to 50% of your income. While that's definitely on the extreme side of things, Pete is just another example of how it can be done.

Granted, the more you make the larger a percentage you can save. The point here is to make some steep sacrifices so that you can put more of your wealth toward investments that are right for you.

Earn Much, Much More.

As the old saying goes: "You have to have money to make money." I know what you're thinking though: "Well Jeff, I don't have any money, so how can I make money if I have no money?"
First, let's address something. When you say that you don't have any money and believe that, you're already setting yourself up for failure. You have to change your mindset and believe that you can find a way to make more money.

5. Work Hard Now

When I think back to how I was able to advance my career, I remember when I was an unpaid intern at the brokerage firm that ended up hiring me. As an intern, I was working 12 to 15 hours a week, showing up when I was told to show up, dressed, and ready to impress. The majority of my duties were shredding important documents, filing, and other basic administrative duties.

Even though the work was boring, I did everything that was asked of me and above. My work ethic and drive spoke for itself. After that summer internship, I was offered a full-time position. If you have a job, even though you might not like that job, give it everything that you've got. Treat the company that you work for as if you own it. Imagine then that you're the CEO. How would you approach your daily duties differently if more was on the line?

It's really difficult to find great opportunities. It's possible, but it isn't easy. For now, I recommend that you focus on working hard. People around you will start to take notice.
Just like I was offered a full-time position because I worked hard as an intern, you will find doors of opportunity opening for you when you give your work all you have.

6. Invest in Your Education

Another way that you might be able to make more is to invest in your education. This could be getting your degree, getting an MBA, or getting a specialized designation. For me, getting my CERTIFIED FINANCIAL PLANNER™ certification has yielded thousands of dollars of revenues over the years.

When I first passed the exam for my certification, many people asked me, "Congratulations, does this mean that you get a raise?" There was no immediate financial benefit for me. It was a year out of my life where I studied my butt off, but I knew having that designation would give me the education and also the credentials to set myself apart from the competition.

While I didn't see any immediate financial benefit, I can attribute several new clients as well as several media opportunities to the fact that I'm Jeff Rose, CFP®. You can get your certification, too!

7. Invest in Yourself and Your Marketing

Over and above that, I have invested into myself. When I was first starting off, I didn't have a lot of money, but I knew I needed to look the part, so I bought fresh shirts, ties, suits – anything I could to make myself look more like a professional. I also invested into personalized brochures, seminars, and other marketing materials to put myself out there.

Another way I invest in myself is by paying $8,900 per year for Strategic Coach – a coaching program with workshops, program advisors, and like-minded entrepreneurs. Dan Sullivan of Strategic Coach has created a program I've found hugely beneficial to my business – my business has grown as a result of his work. Many of his quotes like this one pack a punch:

"For a company to grow 10x, it doesn't need you managing – it needs self-managing."

I always made sure that I didn't overextend myself to where I was spending more than I could afford. A lot of the money that I earned wasn't going toward frivolous things such as big screen TVs or going out to eat at high-end restaurants. Instead, the money went toward investing into myself and my business.

8. Venture into Entrepreneurship

I highly recommend you start building wealth by venturing into entrepreneurship.

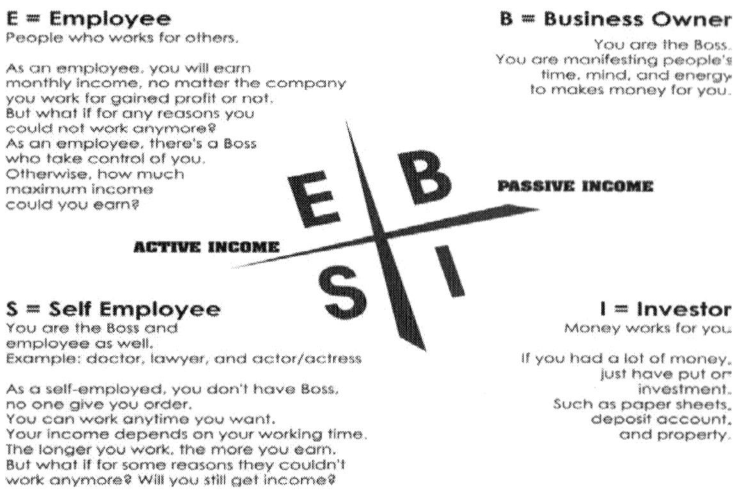

When I became an entrepreneur, my wealth-building journey really took off. Several years prior, I had read the book Rich Dad, Poor Dad. In that book, author Robert Kiyosaki introduces the concept of the cash flow quadrant. He looks at four different entities: the employee, the self-employed, the business owner, and the investor.

When I read that book, I fell under the employee quadrant, but I knew that if I ever wanted to make serious money, I had to get into the right type of quadrant – either the business owner or the investor quadrant (the investor quadrant is actually the best).

When I first started as a financial advisor, I was still an employee. I had the ability to make my own hours and to grow my business as much as I could, but I also had a lot of restrictions.

BiggerPockets.com just how quickly real estate investing can help individuals build wealth. Here's what he had to say:
"Real estate investing may not make you wealthy overnight, but it can add zeros to your net worth in a shorter timeframe than many other traditional investments. For example, purchasing a fixer-upper house, rehabbing the property, and selling it for more can net you a significant windfall if you do it correctly. Just be sure to buy low, rehab smart, and sell fast. House flipping, as this process is called, is largely a math game, and significant profits can be made by those willing to take on the challenge."

Another strategy that can help you add wealth quickly through real estate is by purchasing multifamily properties that produce significant monthly cash flow. This cash flow can be saved and reinvested into more deals, creating a domino effect that will allow you to exponentially grow your real estate portfolio. For more information, read The Ultimate Beginner's Guide to Real Estate Investing from BiggerPockets.com.

Concluding Thoughts on Building Wealth Fast

To build wealth really fast, you're not going to get there by investing $50 to $100 per month into a Roth IRA. While yes, it's great as a long-term strategy, it's not going to make a difference in the short-term. A lot of financial advisers I talked to don't want to encourage you to take that risk now. Heck, I was one of those financial advisors several years ago.

While not letting you know about all the wealth-building options isn't financial malpractice, it's certainly better if your financial advisor gives you a variety of options based on your financial goals – even when it doesn't help his pocketbook. It's always a good idea to talk to several professional investors to see what has worked for them. The best question you can ask any financial professional is how they are investing their money – it will speak volumes.

Let's step back for a moment. You might be thinking: "How in the world can I learn and do all this stuff? Is it even possible?" Don't think that you have to do everything. Instead, focus on a few things and do them well. It all starts by investing in yourself. Listen to podcasts, read books, take millionaires out for lunch (yes, you buy).

You can start by subscribing to an excellent podcast by Lewis Howes: The School of Greatness Podcast. There, you will become equipped to think differently about yourself and your wealth. It's fantastic.

As you make it a habit to find ways to better yourself, you'll also find new potential ways to build wealth faster than ever. Everyone does it differently, and nobody will do it exactly like you. You're unique and you'll find a way. Just give yourself a chance! I'm so glad I gave myself a chance to succeed. You will be too.

CHAPTER
TEN

Summing Things Up

Even if you're not the type to chase wealth, you'd probably say yes to financial comfort. That feeling of not having to think about money — or the more typical reality, stress over it — is what we're all really after.

Whether you ever get to breathe that sigh of relief depends not on the next lottery drawing or get-rich opportunity, but on a combination of your circumstances and your approach to managing your finances. Admittedly, some of those circumstances may be beyond your control. But how you approach the money you have, however limited it may be, is not.

Here are some of my final thoughts, insights, and suggestions about saving and investing:

1. Use Your Time Wisely; Learn the Time Value of Money
Let's consider three people who have $10,000 a year to invest. The first — we'll call her Strong-Start-Samantha — begins investing that $10,000 at age 25 and continues for 10 years. The

second person, Consistent-Cathy, starts saving at age 35 but keeps it up until age 65, without skipping a beat. Finally, Perfect-Penny "one-ups" them both by contributing that $10,000 every year from age 25 to age 65.

It's not hard to figure out that Penny comes out on top here: She puts away more money over a longer time horizon. What may come as a surprise though is that Cathy, who saves $200,000 more than Samantha ends up with a balance that is only about $35,000 higher despite having invested over the course of 30 years.

For that, Samantha can thank—Cathy can curse—compound interest. The longer your money has to grow, the more you end up with and the less you actually have to save. Investment returns start to multiply over time and pick up the slack.

2. Spend Less Than You Earn

You've heard people tell you to live within your means. They're wrong. To really build wealth, you need to live below your means — preferably about 15 percent below.

That's about how much you should be saving for retirement each year (though it's worth determining a more personalized goal by using a retirement calculator), which leaves us with some simple math: If you want to save that much, you need to spend that much less than you make.

While the math is easy, the commitment to spending less is not. It requires an ongoing value judgment: Is this purchase today more important than retirement tomorrow? If it isn't, try to pass.

It also requires avoiding high-interest-rate debt, which can effectively wipe out any chance you have of saving enough—and almost always indicates you're living too large for your budget.

3. Progressively Raise the Bar

If you can save early and consistently like Penny, you get lots of head pats. The rest of us need a more reasonable approach: Start small with whatever you have to save, and then regularly increase that amount. Doing so once a year is great; more frequently is even better.

Getting a raise is a good time to do it, as is after you've paid off a large debt. Direct that extra money toward savings and you won't miss it. Every step counts.

4. Use Every Advantage

Aside from the obvious benefit of saving for retirement—that eternal hammock at the end—there are ongoing benefits, too. If you use the right accounts, you can lap up free money and lower your taxes. Appealing, right?

That free money comes if you're fortunate enough to have an employer plan like a 401(k) that offers matching contributions. Those dollars are an instant return on your investment. If you contribute 6% of your salary, for example, your employer might kick in 3%... and now, you're saving 9% of your income.

The money you put into a 401(k) also reduces your taxable income for the year, thus, lowering the taxes you pay. You're not actually avoiding taxes. In fact, you're just pushing them down the road when you'll pay taxes on distributions from the account in retirement.

If you don't have a 401(k), consider an individual retirement account. A traditional IRA has the same tax treatment as a standard 401(k)—tax break now, pay taxes later—while a Roth IRA works in the reverse: You don't get a tax break now, but you also don't pay taxes on retirement distributions. You can compare Roth and traditional IRAs to see which account makes sense for your situation.

5. Don't Try Too Hard

Can you stock-trade your way to retirement? Sure, but you could also just sit back, relax, and let mutual funds do the work—specifically, low-cost index funds or exchange-traded funds, which track a benchmark index, such as the Standard & Poor's 500. These funds are like baskets that hold small pieces of many different individual investments, which means you get instant diversification, lowering your risk, but typically, not your returns. You can build a solid portfolio out of just four funds, and while you may not beat the market, you should be able to easily keep pace.

ABOUT THE AUTHOR

Ms. Ashaunda' Davis is a financial advisor and speaker who coaches workshop clients in establishing a financial foundation. This establishes the groundwork upon which they can build a clear and concise plan that leads them to their desired financial goals. Ashaunda believes in a holistic, comprehensive, and goal-focused wealth-building and coaching system because traditional financial planning has not sufficiently impacted middle to high income Americans. Thus, it adds to the already perpetuated lack of financial literacy and the implementation of wealth accumulation.

Ashaunda is on a mission to positively impact the financial trajectory of at least 8,000 families across the United States, challenging them to a life of financial stewardship.

Testimonials

"Ms. Ashaunda Davis has opened my eyes to a variety of solutions that will make my money work for me. She is very attentive, and she provided helpful information based on my current needs. Speaking with Ashaunda Davis was the first time I really understood the different insurance options and how to strategically put a plan in place for the future. I really appreciate your help."

C. McWhorter – Managing Attorney

"Ashaunda made me look at the numbers, and that was the hardest part, but that helped the most. Call her now!"

A. Staples Radio Personality

"After working with Ashaunda for a year, I can truly see a positive change in mindset concerning money. I am more equipped to manage my finances appropriately for a sounder future."

Dr. Cambri Gregg, PT, DPT

"I absolutely love the tips and changes Financial Advisor Ashaunda Davis has taught me. Genuine person that cares means a lot to me especially when the subject can be sensitive."

Deliqua Isom - Master Personal Trainer, Life Coach

"All great teams have a great coach. I'm more financially confident than ever thanks to my coach, Ashaunda!"

D. Swearingen, Entrepreneur

"Ashaunda has the unique ability to customize a plan that works for your family. As a coach, she gives you the game plan to a more financially abundant life."

J. Wright-Jennings, Mortgage Branch Manager